sparrow

also by dan knapp

a handful of fragments

sparrow

by dan knapp

each day i watch
for the little brown sparrow
brings hope for the day
and maybe the morrow

INFINITY
PUBLISHING.COM

Copyright © 2009 by dan knapp

ISBN 0-7414-5203-0

All written selections, photography, graphics and cover design by dan knapp

Published by:

INFINITY
PUBLISHING.COM
1094 New DeHaven Street, Suite 100
West Conshohocken, PA 19428-2713
Info@buybooksontheweb.com
www.buybooksontheweb.com
Toll-free (877) BUY BOOK
Local Phone (610) 941-9999
Fax (610) 941-9959

Printed in the United States of America
Printed on Recycled Paper
Published February 2009

to my mother, father and sister

~Acknowledgements ~

I wish to extend my gratitude to those who were instrumental
in the development of this project.
For your generosity, words of encouragement, and support
I Thank You
Donna Derrig ~ Ed Osgood ~ Tim McBride

In addition, I extend my appreciation to

INFINITY
PUBLISHING.COM

For their consideration and sincerity
in making this project a reality
and a pathway of hope
through the night

contents

contents ∘——

preface

It's early December and this past weekend ushered in some the coldest temperatures of the season so far. Blustery winds and snow showers accentuated the rawness of the wintry weather as a preview of what may lie ahead during the next several months. Brown leaves left behind from the colorful show of autumn swirled about the yard and huddled beneath the spruce and pine trees. Green yards and fields had turned brown for the winter and the absence of birds, squirrels or rabbits or any other wildlife made up the desolate view. Even the woodchuck that has a burrow behind the garage didn't emerge from the comforts of its den to check out the day's activities and nibble on the remnants of grass and clover. Raucous blue jays and crows that live in the woodlot were unusually quiet. Most likely, they were trying to keep sheltered from the bone chilling gusts of wind as well. Toward the end of the day, while glancing out the window, I saw a house sparrow perched on a branch of the juniper bush. The little brown bird sat motionless with its feathers puffered out for warmth and protection from the biting cold wind and freezing rain.

Seeing a sparrow in the yard at this time of year was somewhat unusual and I wondered whether it was lost and unable to find its way home. Throughout the remainder of the day, I thought about the sparrow and hoped it would survive the blast of cold weather. Nightfall seemed to arrive a bit earlier as snow clouds passed overhead on the blanket of grey sky. The last time I saw the sparrow in the dusky light, it was still sitting on a branch of the juniper bush – motionless with all of its feathers puffered out.

After going to bed for the night, I slipped under the covers and listened to the persistent wind rushing through stark tree branches. Sleep was elusive and I finally conceded to failed attempts of falling asleep sometime around 3 a.m. I went to the living room to read for a while but had difficulty concentrating on the book I had chosen. Needless to say, the night was brief and didn't allow for much rest. The quiet early morning hours that followed were marked by the ticking clock on the wall and the ebb and flow of the dogs' breathing as they slept beside the chair. The minutes between the chimes of the clock seemed to be passing by at half-speed and anticipating the light of daybreak only seemed to prolong the minutes and hours all the more. For reasons unknown, the little sparrow remained in my thoughts and I hoped to see it sitting in the juniper bush when darkness gave way to the morning light.

Eventually, the sun slowly began to rise above the horizon. It was quite a pleasant sight to see the sparrow still perched in the juniper and to know that it had endured the harsh weather throughout the night. The little bird basked in the warm sunlight, stretching its wings and preening its feathers for a short time before it flew away, presumably, to search for its home.

Like the sparrow, some may stray from the home where we feel at ease in the company of familiar people in a familiar setting. The old adage of 'home is where the heart is' succinctly describes what makes up a home. Wealth and material possessions do not make one home a better place to live than another. Rather, a home is where love, peace and contentment emanate from the hearts and souls of those who are caring and understanding of their loved ones while they are living together harmoniously.

Oddly, when the words of the familiar saying are switched to that of 'a heart is where the home is' it maintains significant meaning. Most everyone has a place in their heart where they can go when difficult times fall upon them and feel that this is where they need to be and belong for the time being. It's a place of self acceptance, appreciation and understanding. The home of the heart is a place where one can go for comfort as well as for comforting. It's a place of refuge where one would unconditionally welcome his own soul and feel at ease during the visit. Some are blessed with the ability of finding the home in their heart with ease while others may travel the world or spend a lifetime searching for their heart's home ~ that place of peace and contentment.

While having a morning cup of coffee, thoughts of the sparrow resurfaced piquing my curiosity about the significance of the event. Why the recurrence of thoughts about the sparrow? What piece of information was missing? What was the meaning behind all of this? I came to the conclusion that perhaps this was to remind me of the strength of hope by my wanting to see the "sparrow in the morning light". This hope or desire, in turn, became a pathway through the night.

I hope that by sharing my thoughts and imagery of "sparrow", will, in some way, convey my empathy as well as provide some moments of respite for anyone who may be going through difficult times. But, more importantly, I hope that "sparrow" will shine a light on your hopes that become a pathway to get you through the night and help you find your way home.

May your heart feel the comforts of home

dan

hope

when will come the day
little bird of hope
you'll find your way
my heart can be your home
we'll both feel less alone

beginnings

i'm tired of it
my spirit for life is numb
the hollow in my heart
fills with uncertainties
i can't help but wonder
how much longer can i endure
is there no key for the door

dreams and aspirations
once held in my eyes
are now smoldering heaps of ash
they're gone
there's not much hope
for salvaging the remains
there's not much hope
for rebuilding yet again
for all it will ever be
is just dust in the wind.

contentment is a star
of the velvet night sky
so many times
i wanted to reach for it
to touch it to hold it
to feel it's light inside me.
but in reality i know
that's not going happen
not now not ever

chasing shadows

i dreamed i saw you
in calico fields of flowers last night
sweet child of innocence
chasing stray shadows
in the pale moonlight

i thought i heard you
in the whispering wind last night
your comforting voice
faint and fading
until lost in silence

i dreamed you held me
in your arms last night
your tenderness
warm and gentle
like candlelight

i dreamed my heart
found its way home last night
but these dreams
are just shadows
i keep chasing

the vacant lot

it's late november
daylight has grown colder
dusk settles in with a damp chill

a sunset of golden light
flaring from the horizon
casts ember shades across the sky
rose and lavender ash
blush billowing clouds
slipping into the night

fog drapes its shroud over the vacant lot
a special place where we used to go
spent queen anne's lace and goldenrod flowers
surreal like
float on lofty greyness

there's a craggy old apple tree
standing off kilter on a grassy knoll
from its branch hangs a broken rope swing
it stirs with the slightest breeze
like a pendulum for times now gone

sometimes distant sometimes unclear
haunting voices of innocence
fill the raw air
yet no one goes there anymore

as darkening clouds thicken
they can hold back no longer
and begin to weep wintry weather
cold tears run down my face
when i think of those times
will never be replaced

baseball on the sill

in that old tattered house
ragged sheer curtains hang limp
behind broken panes of glass
and the cockeyed front door won't stay shut
the green tarpapered roof sags
from bearing the weight of so many years

there's an empty room
in the far back corner
it has a worn plank floor
and black scuffs speckle
cold off-white bare walls
a dusty brown cowboy hat
lies propped up in the corner
some young boy
must have lived here once before

rays of sunlight
streak through hazy glass
from opaque shafts
crooked shadows are cast
obliquely stretching
from the sill across the floor
seemingly searching
to escape through the door

someone from some forgotten time
left a baseball on the window sill
yellowed and cracked enamel
peels from the dry rotted frame
hardened window glazing
barely holds rattling panes

the brown bruised leather ball
with a recent grass stain
precariously placed on the ledge
recalls all those years gone by
and every baseball game
and every boy who threw it in play
who left it there
and why would they do that anyway?

age faded red stitches
broken and frayed
the seam has split wide open
and the leather curls away
so much older i've become
so much has been wasted along the way
and the baseball on the window sill
awaits another day

wetlands

mirrored in shallow black glass
near water's edge
slanting pine skeletons
stand still

branches chaotically meshed
sketched pen and ink
barren silhouettes
on painted sunset skies

diffused light of dusk
through haze of a late day storm
illuminates strands of fog
hovering over quiescent water

night noises swell
in concert with droning cicadas
while flickering fireflies
quietly appear

thorn apple

quince

october night

if only to be
a silvery star
shining bright
to silently steal away
among the shadows
of the crescent moonlight

lost star in the sky
brightly burned out tonight
too soon to expire
on this october night

while stargazers are scoping
constellations and galaxies
and astronomers
try to find the archer's arrow

i'm freefalling
from the darkness
that once made me shine bright
only to become a dark star
and shine with dark light

empty branch
if only to be like the sparrow
i think i would fly away too

seasons

with awakenings of spring
i learned the lyrics of love
but i don't sing them anymore
all too often
on deaf ears they have fallen
now, love's a stranger at my door

in sunsets of summer
we walked the dusty dirt road
to the field where we used to play
sometimes we picked
wild red strawberries
hiding in sweet clover and hay

calicoed hills of autumn leaves
burst in blazes of colors
glowing like embers
in shades of red orange and yellow
like the warmth from your heart
i long to remember

wintry weather blusters in
with a dusting of snow overnight
black capped chickadees flit about
on branches of the sycamore tree
listen while they sing the lyrics of love
for someone else to learn
with awakenings of spring

misty cove

dusty rose at daybreak
with golden light shine
reflecting from grey clouds
hues of lavender light

ripped ragged the shoreline
and black branched spears
pierce through muted colors
so ominous yet so peaceful

in murky shallows
a blue heron wades
then stands frozen
in gradients of jade

as waters deepen
and change to black shades
on the rippling surface
rough cut diamonds
sparkle and fade

fog hovering low
quiets restless water
for you to behold
this watercolor

gladiolus

just you and me on the front porch swing
remember when we painted it forest green
gladiolus bouquets and sweetened lemonade
we'd sit for hours reminiscing the good old days

so many years we loved each other
so many years we were one
and, now it seems like forever
since the day you've been gone

i loved your laughter
you comforted my heart
i miss you dearly
and hope i did my part

this spring past
we planted your flowers
winter hearts were warmed
with your loving touch
and gentle april showers

graceful leaves of jade
growing in the summer shade
concealing the flowers
that would burst into colors

i touch you in every petal
your laughter is every color
it feels like you're here with me
you are my flower

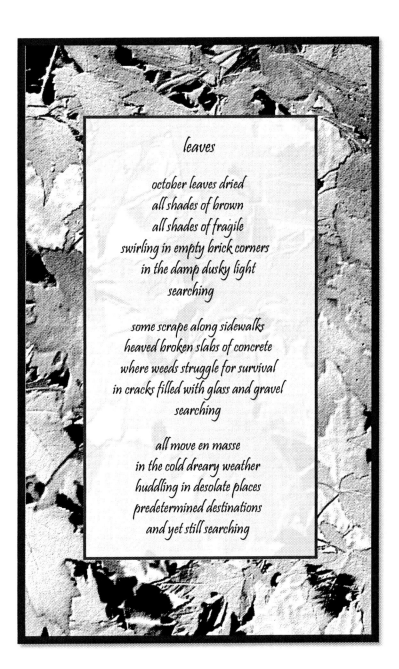

leaves

october leaves dried
all shades of brown
all shades of fragile
swirling in empty brick corners
in the damp dusky light
searching

some scrape along sidewalks
heaved broken slabs of concrete
where weeds struggle for survival
in cracks filled with glass and gravel
searching

all move en masse
in the cold dreary weather
huddling in desolate places
predetermined destinations
and yet still searching

insipid insanity

so
i guess this is it

this is where i'll be
bearing witness
to this insipid insanity

time drags or seems to stand still
have all the clocks locked up
has the pendulum stilled
anxiously waiting
from the shallow of each breath
will the next one follow
or was that the last
has my time come to pass

no desires have i
nor expectations
i portend no intent
absolutions or convictions
no more living in silence
no more

in this exercise of futility
blindly believing lies and deceit
trust is compromised
integrity fractured
virtues scrutinized
breaking the branches of humanity

where is honor and humility
truth
compassion
hope

the light of hope fades

i wish i could smile
and feel it in my heart.
i wish i could laugh so hard
there would be tears of joy
not hurt
i wish i could feel loved
and love someone so dear
i wish i could live life
outside this darkness
of fear

for love knows not of me

when you say i love you
in my heart i don't understand
i don't know how to feel loved
i don't know if i can

when love wilts and fades away
and leaves you feeling forsaken
tears that bleed from a broken heart
won't bring it back again

when you say i love you
i ask how can that be
whose reflection is in your eyes
for love knows not of me

savor the flavor of love
for it nourishes the heart and soul

tend your garden

tend the garden of your soul
let the flowers awaken
for they will bloom
bouquets of colors
let them fill the emptiness
hurting
has left in your heart

_____

_____

_____

_____

_____

_____

_____

_____

_____

_____

_____

_____

_____

_____

she
will bend you
to the brink
of snapping
like a twig
then
just leave you
hanging there

she loves me
she loves me not

dogma

i'm tired
so very tired
if only this would end
now

i can't cry it out
or scream it out
i'm black and white
all my colors have bled out

i feel apart
broken and scattered
not much is left
as the remnants unravel

love's a stranger
hope is nebulous
where is the light
for these days of darkness

i'm tired
so very tired
where can i go
when i've no place
i can call home

circus mirrors

yellow lights blinking and blue cotton candy
circus barkers for surreal side shows
bearded lady, fortune teller, the alligator man
fake or for real? who knows but them
yet the far away look in our eyes
ask where do we belong

caught in a labyrinth of circus mirrors
indiscernible reflections surround me
i don't think there's a way out of here
and
these hallucinations seem like reality

faceless images staring back at me
melting like dali's imagery
they listen but they don't hear
they look but they don't see
they're munch's man screaming
just like me

among these images i cannot recognize
which are reflections and which one is me
are they simply illusions of my mind's eye
how can i know which one is me

jigsaw

something inside me has died
or maybe it was just never alive
i've wept until there's nothing left
then replenished with loneness and discontent

i've tried to make sense of it all
but some things make no sense at all
is this journey one without end
it seems i've been down this road
and back again
i keep going around in circles
the wheel of life
but living without purpose?

why won't these damn pieces fit
why are there so many missing
where should i look
where are the lost ones
will this jigsaw puzzle ever be done

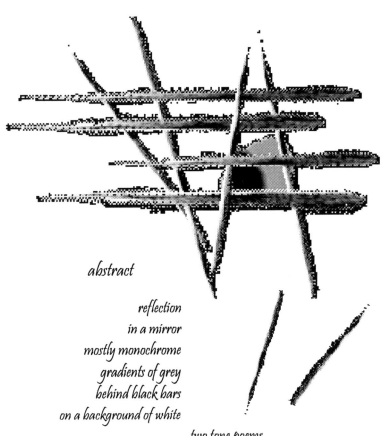

abstract

reflection
in a mirror
mostly monochrome
gradients of grey
behind black bars
on a background of white

two tone poems
express emotions
one of indigo
one of sienna
perspectives
have no points of reference
no shadows or projections
nor source of light
on this canvas is painted
my still life

city streets

still wet from the rain
reflections are drawn taut
as shiny neon streaks
across black patent leather streets

metal and glass serpents
slither over coal black ice
red eyes ever vigilant
red eyes that never sleep

one is sitting on a bench
profiled in red yellow then green
red yellow then green
red yellow then green
how many times?
sixteen or seventeen
or so it seems

an other one is standing
on another corner
flickering in mercurial day light
an indefinable extension
of an outstretched shadow
absorbed into the night

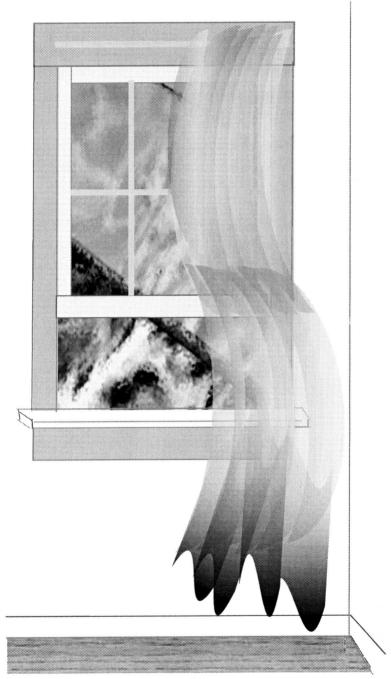

13

life on a canvas
    is nothing more than
    painted grey skies
        with bleakness sketched
    in graphite and charcoal

suspended animation

should i go another way
i won't ask for understanding
for i no longer question reasons
i only know i don't belong
and no longer should i stay

i've lost all sense of direction
i'm not sure which way to turn
drifting through these caverns and canyons
i keep searching for someplace
a place where i belong

such a fool i've been
such a damn fool for believing
to think i would ever know love again
or think it would ever know me
what a damned fool i've been to believe

it's not easy to have faith anymore
or hold on to hope
what holy house of inspiration
would welcome such a faithless fool
among its congregation

why are all the doors locked
and every exit blocked
there's no way in
and there's no way out
in between i live my life in doubt

bare wires

bare ends of frayed wires
spark blue arcs of electricity
like synapses short circuiting
burning holes in my brain

patched with generic caplets
and easy to swallow bandages
you know ~
those temporary fixes
for those
permanent damages

am i that far gone
that far beyond repair
i feel so damn much out of place
makes me wonder
should anything be salvaged
from this oddity of the human race

i believe that i don't belong here
i'm convinced ~ i feel it in my gut
i don't think i'll ever get out of here
for every door down the hall
has been slammed shut

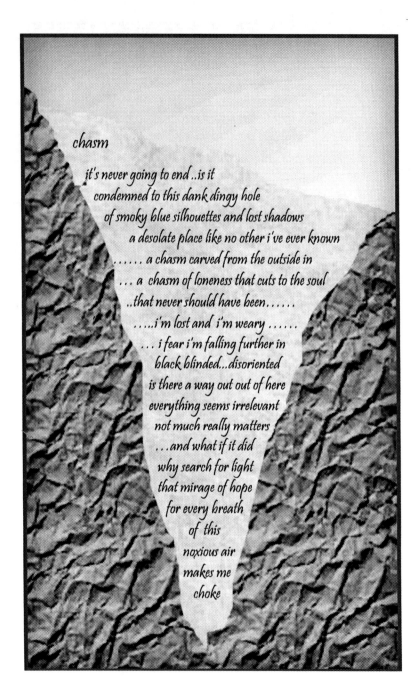

chasm

it's never going to end ..is it
condemned to this dank dingy hole
of smoky blue silhouettes and lost shadows
a desolate place like no other i've ever known
...... a chasm carved from the outside in
... a chasm of loneness that cuts to the soul
..that never should have been......
.....i'm lost and i'm weary ......
... i fear i'm falling further in
black blinded...disoriented
is there a way out out of here
everything seems irrelevant
not much really matters
...and what if it did
why search for light
that mirage of hope
for every breath
of this
noxious air
makes me
choke

wind and currents

adrift on these uncharted waters
i go where the wind and currents carry me
endlessly drifting
drifting aimlessly
knowing not where fate is taking me

my homeland shores are distant
far beyond what my eyes can see
i fear i'll never walk those shores again
or find my home of peace and tranquility

gone are the days i've longed to remember
gone with those i've forgotten
and all those forgotten yesterdays
fill tomorrows with nothing

this sea worn skiff is what i've got
mostly white dappled with driftwood grey
the rudder won't work and one oar's lost
the hull leaks from its peeling paint

nothing but sea surrounds me
as i endlessly drift under starry skies
drifting aimlessly
as the wind and currents carry me

the traveler

at one with his soul
walking along a broken path
a weary traveler is he
determined yet without direction
no place is his home
his steps are slowed and deliberate
as if keeping in time to
with a dirge metronome
there's a lost look in his eyes
while searching cloudless skies
only to face the reality
there's no other place he should be

a lone sparrow perching on hemlocks
leads him through the grassy meadow
nearby lies a beckoning woodlot
a cathedral of tranquility
stained glass windows of autumn leaves
graced with columns of oak and maple trees
and forest sounds sing in sweet harmony
what pleasure to behold
this secret place of beauty and mystery

milky rays of the late day sun
slice through corridors lined with trees
white greylight beyond the horizon
sheds light on shadows now stretched thin
the forest is much less foreboding
its darkness much less frightening

soon the day wears old
and lets the sun slip away
the traveler's silhouette fades
as he goes further into the woods
i wonder if i could follow him
or even if i should
i wonder where is he going
or if he knows where he's been
and if i shouldn't follow
he may never pass this way again

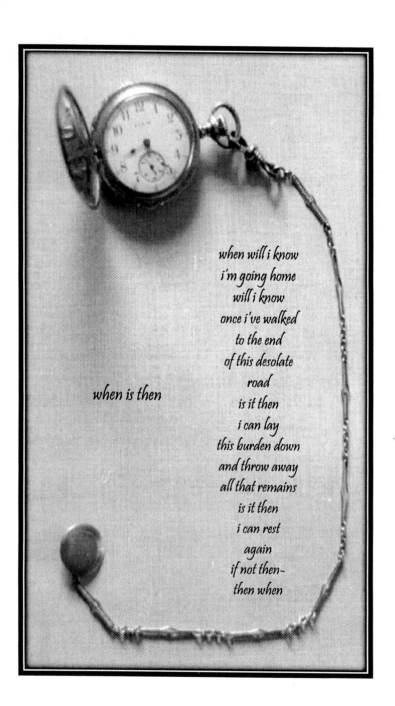

when is then

when will i know
i'm going home
will i know
once i've walked
to the end
of this desolate
road
is it then
i can lay
this burden down
and throw away
all that remains
is it then
i can rest
again
if not then-
then when

lost

stillness surrounds me
like fog on a cold damp day
so much greyness around me
as i drift even further away

no longer can i see
the homeland shores
that once harbored me
and, now i don't know
the man i used to be

trust has been broken
i've no reason to carry on
for now i know for certain
i'll never belong

whatever happened
what went wrong
where is hope
when all else is gone

lost is the soul
that was my identity
so i'll set sail with the clouds
and let the wind carry me

tell me

tell me of some dreams
for i have none of my own
what is it that you see
where do you go

tell me about hope
peace and contentment
will any of these
open this prison of torment

tell me about a love
that ends a heart's yearning
a love that feeds the hunger
and soothes the soul's hurting

i've grown tired and weary
what once was is now gone
tell me the way home
for no longer do i know
which way i should go

i am but a foreigner

sometimes
in shadowed light
i feel helpless
as i stand witness
to the slow dissolve of my soul
erosion permeates my being
like cancer consumes flesh
is there no cure
to heal this hurt

how do i salvage
some degree of integrity
it's not easy understanding
the person i've come to be
i'm not certain of who i am
or what's become of my identity
where will i go
what will i be

i am but a foreigner
lost in my own land
with hopeless ideations
loneness and isolation
all gouged with abandon
to the depths of my being

questions

i feel uncentered
i live a life out of balance
i live in the cellars of reality
and can't find the one i used to be
whatever happened to my identity
tell me of peace and contentment
or if they even exist
tell me of true happiness
what's it like to be out of this darkness
my arms have grown tired
my legs are too weak to walk
i can't withstand much more of this
enough is enough
how far must one travel
this dismal road with no end
are the answers found along the way
or do they lie just beyond the horizon
how far must one travel
until he's found his road's end
an eye for an eye
for this disease of desperation
just as metal turns to rust
i've become depression
think not of me as cowardly
for surrendering in silence
rather one who has conquered
his enemy of persistence

you can come in . . .

      . . . but you cannot stay

through the tree leaf canopy
with a background of blue sky
bright sunlight sparkles
with glimpses of clouds roving by

hemlock trees and dried brown leaves
mossy bark fiddler ferns and fertile loam
decaying wood of fallen trees
i felt like i was part of each of these
i felt like i was home

ancient stones
split slabbed and broken
blotched with velvety moss
 and patches of blue-green lichen
aimlessly float in sepia toned leaves
among oases of sparse forest greenery

three sparrow fledglings
perched on hickory twigs
stretching tiny wings
gaping mouths opened wide
each anxiously waiting
for the first to take flight

the sentry crow's caw
announces day's end is near
as golden clouds turn silver
and twilight stars appear
it was then i heard
the slightest breeze whisper
this is your home
there's a place for you here

when i close my eyes

when i close my eyes
let the light within keep shining
shine like a star in bible black skies
let it keep shining

behind these eyes light is fading
obscured by clouds of confusion
paled by blue moonlight waning
why all of this damned disillusion

when i close my eyes
let the light within shine
shine like a beacon
and guide me through this night

fog

silently fog creeps in
on the coattails of nor' easterly winds
a flowing cloud that's gone astray
floating on the placid lake
filling in hollows as it slides over hills

in time, all is immersed
in the rawness of this season
cold rains chill to the bone
and the thick blanket of white
offers no warmth or comfort

whitewashed and faded colors
signal not many days linger
before fall gives way
to frost of wintry weather

dim rays of blue light
stretching from street lamps
glow on ghosts of buildings
and stark mangled branches
so solemn is the sparrow
perched in the sleeping lilac
on such a dismal day

sagging power lines
between shrinking poles
trail off in the shadowed white
where silhouettes appear
and shadows disappear
as if keeping in sync
with the balance of life

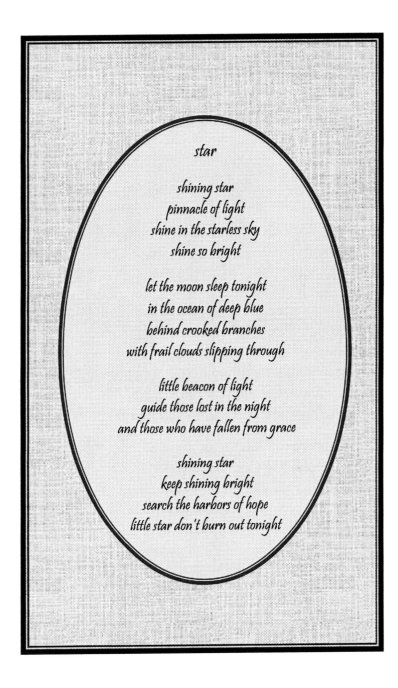

star

shining star
pinnacle of light
shine in the starless sky
shine so bright

let the moon sleep tonight
in the ocean of deep blue
behind crooked branches
with frail clouds slipping through

little beacon of light
guide those lost in the night
and those who have fallen from grace

shining star
keep shining bright
search the harbors of hope
little star don't burn out tonight

the visitor

i thought i saw you last night
as i turned out the parlor light
moonbeams swept across the floor
and shadowed tree branches on the wall
you were sitting in that chair
right over there
just like you used to do before

i watched you sleeping peacefully
hypnotized by your breathing
i breathed every breath with you
for a moment
i felt as if i was with you
i felt renewed
but only for a moment
before that feeling was gone

your sleeping eyes spoke of serenity
your soft hair framed contentment
your presence filled every room
of this empty old house
maybe it was a dream
that made you smile twice
maybe it was your way of showing
you knew i was there

soft darkness warmed the room
and the shadows melted from the wall
as the moon stole behind
a silver lined cloud
i thought i saw you last night
but only for a moment
when i turned ~
you were gone

grey skies and no shadows

a black bird takes wing
this damp december morning
his silhouetted flight
journeys with snow clouds
bulging and backlit with golden light

like a fisherman's knotted net
tree branches entangle and mesh
as they span evening skies painted grey
just as the skiff's hull i'm empty
i've no catch for the day

restless river of clouds
endlessly flows in silence above
until the weary sojourner
empties stolen shadows and borrowed light
into seas of starless nights

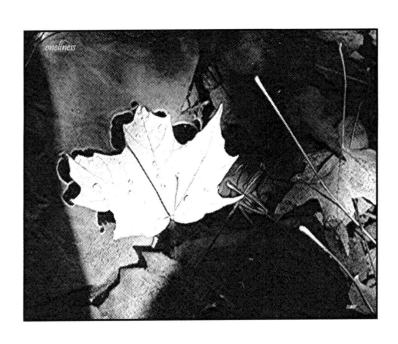

oneliness

old brown boots

broken down leather
stiff scuffed and forlorn
the heels are well rounded
to the extent they've been worn

frayed and knotted bootlaces
used to drag along the ground
seems like they'd always trip me up
and sometimes make me fall down

once repaired by a cobbler
when the sole was worn through
and the first last didn't
and the left heel came unglued

now mildewed and musty
with a tongue that's dog chewed
there's still a hole in one sole
and the other one just flaps loose

how many miles have they traveled
does it matter where they've been
what ground have they covered
whose shit have they stepped in

the boots have served their purpose
so someone just tossed them aside
most likely they'll never be worn again
as if they're suspended in time

over there in the blank corner
beside the wood bench they lie
the left one still stands upright
the other is on its side

tired eyes
his eyes look tired
his smile weary
his haggard face
that's weathered harsh years
is chiseled with lines of character
and scarred by sorrow and despair

haunted by ghostly dreams
that have been long since gone
whisper how much older he's become
he seems so fragile so solemn
and moves as if he's made of porcelain

a frail silhouette cast from winter light
shuffles toward the empty parlor
there, in the amber lit corner
a winged back chair awaits
the one with the brown throw cover

he nestles in familiar warmth and comfort
as he rests in the bosom of his chair
tired eyes blankly stare into space
yet see nothing here
on the chair side table his broken glasses lay
with a dusty handful of fragments
next to the brass lamp base

his heart beats in rhythm
to the mantel clock's ticking
time ticking away time
unending time
as the grand master of thieves
steals back every moment
leaving stilled silence behind

everyone here

everyone here
is with destiny determined
everyone here prepares
from the moment of conception
everyone prepares
throughout their years
for when the time comes
their journey's end draws near

whether it's long lives well blessed
or ones that end in mother's womb
lives shortened by hopelessness
or ones stretched with manmade tools
everyone prepares
and none too soon

            some die from loneness
                some die of fright
                    some die in darkness
                        or when they see light
                    some die the first time
                    others again and again
                        some die slowly
                            with unbearable pain

some die deliberately
some out of desperation
some die with disease
some with holy inspiration
some die suddenly
some lives just cease
some die while living
some die in peace

will there be heaven
or will it be hell
will there be nothing
those who know won't tell

yet everyone here
 without exception
will partake in life's transition
and everyone here
 crosses the threshold alone
for dying is part of living

self portrait
unfinished

a stretched canvas rests
on an easel before me
i've a bristle brush in hand
tabula rasa waiting
in the empty whiteness i see
obscure imagery
the subject of this painting to be
words from life's palette
are the colors i choose
mostly muted vague and obtuse
flesh tones are translucent
sometimes opaque
while the background blends
in gradients of grey
pen and ink hatch marks
fill the void
light has no source of origin
it comes not from outside nor within
no shadows are cast
revealing depth or emotion
only shades of colors
with overtones of the past
eyes of polished coal
vacant and hollow
reflecting starless skies
but have none of their own

eyes of the lost
and of those growing old
knowing they don't belong
yet know not where to go
i no longer recognize
this portraiture of my own
colors and textures
bleed and blend
into a ragged tapestry of old
some threads are missing
and some will break
as the warp and weft
disintegrate
among the ash of colors
lies a silhouette of dimension
a composition incused
without compliment
without contrast
a silhouette camouflaged
for protection or isolation
i'll rinse my paintbrush
until the water runs clear
and place it on the easel shelf
for it's now that i have finished
this portrait of myself

mantra

it's going to be ok
believe in your heart
it's going to be ok
hold on to your dreams
let all else slip away
hold on
what's left will be ok

maybe i'll see
through this darkest night
it shouldn't be long 'til dawn
believe
in every darkness there is light
keep holding on
everything will be alright

there's no need to harbor hurt
there's no need at all
just let it go
and feel the light
it's going to be alright
just let it go

little bird

it's been a while
since last i've heard little sparrow
i can't help but wonder
will i hear his song tomorrow

where have you gone
little bird of hope
are you safe from harm
have you found your way

each day i watch and wonder
will you ever come by this way again
has your heart found home
are you gone now forever

hurting hearts shouldn't feel alone

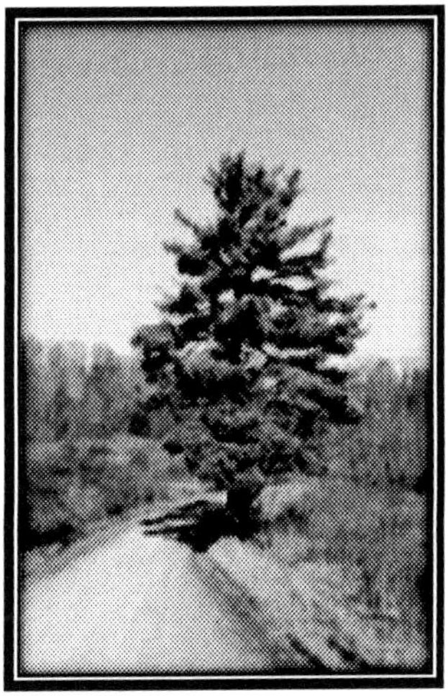